I0560846

PETER, WHO?

THE AMAZING SPIDER-MUSICAL PARODY

SAME POWER, GREATER RESPONSIBILITY
(HIGH SCHOOL EDITION)

BOOK & LYRICS BY
JUSTIN MORAN & JONATHAN ROUFAEAL

MUSIC BY
DOUG KATSAROS & ADAM PODD

Uproar Theatrics

LICENSING & PRODUCTION INQUIRIES
Uproar Theatrics, LLC.
hello@uproartheatrics.com | www.UproarTheatrics.com

Peter, Who?
Book and Lyrics copyright © 2021 byJustin Moran & Jonathan Roufaeal
Music copyright © 2021 by Doug Katsaros & Adam Podd

Peter, Who? is published by Uproar Theatrics, LLC
500 8th Ave FRNT 3, #1714 New York, NY 10018

ISBN: 978-1-968051-34-1

First Printing, May 2025

CAUTION: Professionals and amateurs are hereby warned that all material in this script and libretto, being fully protected under the copyright laws of the United States, the British Empire including the Dominion of Canada, and all other countries of the Copyright Union, is subject to royalty. All rights, including professional, amateur, motion picture, recitation, lecturing, public reading, radio and television broadcasting, and the rights of translation into foreign languages, are strictly reserved. The stock and amateur performance rights in the English language through the United States, its territories and possessions and the rest of the World are controlled exclusively by Uproar Theatrics, LLC., www.UproarTheatrics.com, 500 8th Ave FRNT 3 #1714 New York, NY 10018-4597 No performances of the play may be given without obtaining in advance the written permission of Uproar Theatrics, LLC. and paying the requisite fee. Inquiries concerning all other rights should be directed to Uproar Theatrics, LLC. at the web address stated above.

SPECIAL NOTE: Anyone receiving permission to produce *Peter, Who?* is required to give credit to Justin Moran & Jonathan Roufaeal (book & lyrics) and Doug Katsaros & Adam Podd (music) as sole and exclusive authors of the Play on the title page of all programs distributed in connection with performances of the Play and in all instances in which the title of the Play appears, including printed or digital materials for advertising, publicizing or otherwise exploiting the Play and/or a production thereof. Please see your production license for font size and typeface requirements. It is the licensee's responsibility to ensure any and all required billing is included in the requisite places, per the terms of the license.

Looking for the Album?

You can find it under the musical's original title,
The Spidey Project

CAST OF CHARACTERS

PETER: High school student, nerdy social outcast turned super hero.

GWEN: High school student, polite, charming and gunning for scholarship money.

FLASH: High school student, bully/jock type.

UNCLE BEN: Older man, father figure to Peter

AUNT MAY: Older woman, maternal but independent

KENT HOLBROOK: Fear mongering news reporter with a killer smile

DR. SPIDERMAN: (Pronounced Spidder-min) Crazy old scientist, paranoid and brilliant.

JONAH JAMESON: A brash news chief who is not ashamed of himself and can easily tell you why things were better yesterday.

BETTY: Newspaper secretary, eager and nervous

THE ENSEMBLE (Can be doubled and tripled)

STUDENTS:
KATIE
KAREN
MARVIN KEELY

VILLAINS:
ELECTRO
SCORPION
RHINO
CHAMELEON

EXTRAS:
BANK TELLER
CHIPOTLE WAITER
TV STUDIO WORKERS
MAY'S FRIENDS
THE DOCTOR

THE PLACE

Forest Hills, Queens (New York)

THE TIME

Present Day

<u>MUSICAL NUMBERS</u>

PROLOGUE
Overture . . . . The Band

SCENE 1: A Newsroom / Forest Hills High School
News Opening . . . . .Kent Holbrook
Peter, Who?. . . . . Peter, Flash,
Ensemble
Hurricane Flash . . . . Flash
Peter, Who? (Reprise 1) . . . . Peter

SCENE 2: Aunt May's House
Nice Guys . . . . Aunt May, Peter,
Ensemble

SCENE 4: Subway Platform
Chipotle . . . . Flash, Ensemble

SCENE 5: Science Lab / City Streets
Transformation . . . . Peter

SCENE 7: Uncle Ben's Kitchen
Hero of Men . . . . Uncle Ben

SCENE 8: The City Streets
Who is the Man?. . . . . Ensemble

SCENE 9: Hospital / City Streets
With Great Power . . . . Peter, Ensemble

SCENE 10: Aunt May's House
Hurricane Flash (Reprise) . . . . Flash
Peter Who (Reprise 2) . . . . Peter

SCENE 11: Daily Bugle
Peter, Who? (Reprise 3) . . . . Betty

SCENE 12: Newsroom / City Streets
Killer on the Loose . . . . Kent Holbrook

SCENE 13: The City Streets
Who is the Man? (Reprise) . . . . Ensemble

SCENE 14: Chipotle / Bank
When I Look at You / Villain Song . . . . . Gwen, Electro,
Scorpion
Peter, Who? (Reprise 4) . . . . Peter

SCENE 15: A Rooftop
Face in the Mirror . . . . Chameleon
Chameleon Fight . . . . The Band
Finale (A Little Hope Right Now) . . . . . Company

ACT I

SCENE 1

INT. THE LOCAL CHANNEL 1 NEWSROOM

After the 01. "THE OVERTURE", lights up. The scenery is projected on the back wall like a comic-book panel, it is of a News Room.

KENT HOLBROOK, the fear mongering reporter, is getting ready to broadcast the local Channel One News, he is warming up in his dressing room as assistants are buzzing by.

CAMERA MAN
Thirty seconds till we're live, Kent.

KENT HOLBROOK
(to himself, a vocal warm-up)
EMMY, EMMY, EMMY, EMMY!

You can do this!

ASSISTANT
(running through)
NOT, TILL YOU'RE NATIONAL KENT!

KENT HOLBROOK
EMMY, EMMY, EMMY...

And you're getting married tomorrow!

CAMERA MAN
Going live in five, four, three, two...

Kent hits his mark, someone enters holding an empty 'comic panel', they frame Kent, who is now broadcasting on live TV.

Lights fade to a spotlight on Kent inside the panel, the rest of the stage is dark.

SONG 02. "NEWS OPENING"

KENT HOLBROOK
(singing)
THIS IS KENT HOLBROOK
FROM LOCAL CHANNEL ONE!
PANIC STRIKES OUR BOROUGH
AND WE ALL FEEL THE STING,
EVERYBODY'S KIDS ARE WRAPPED WITH FEAR.
MY NAME IS KENT HOLBROOK, FROM LOCAL
CHANNEL ONE,
AND COLLEGE APPLICATION TIME IS HERE.
SO STOP YOUR TEENS FROM SMOKING,
THEIR FLAGRANT DRUG ABUSE...
FOR TEMPTATION'S ON THE LOOSE!

LIGHTS CROSS-FADE.

INT. HALLWAY OF FOREST HILLS HIGH SCHOOL - DAY

KENT and the others exit while STUDENTS begin to meander on.

The lights fade up on the rest of the stage. The comic-scene panels depict the halls of Forest Hills High School; the students are all a little crazy this time of year. Halls are crowded with

2

people scribbling in notebooks and reviewing note-cards.

KATIE and KAREN are trying to photograph MARVIN KEELY in the hallway for the Yearbook. Marvin is 'the one' for this scene.

SONG 03. "PETER, WHO?"

STUDENTS
OH GOD! THE MID-TERMS START TOMORROW!
MY PARENTS CALL ME A DISGRACE.
THEY ALWAYS LOOK SO DISAPPOINTED...
SOMEONE, SOMEWHERE PUNCH ME IN THE
FACE!

KAREN
Smile for the yearbook! Real smile... is this how you want people to remember you, Marvin Keely? As an ironic smiler?

PETER enters.

KAREN
Peter! I need you to get a quote from Flash Thompson for the yearbook. You know, something great... or whatever... like whatever he normally says. No! No asking questions, just please, just do this! Marvin Keely, I am NOT a patient woman!

STUDENTS
OH GOD! THE MID-TERMS START TOMORROW!
I WANNA RIP MY BRAIN IN HALF.

3

GIRLS
I'D RATHER GIVE A SPEECH TO CONGRESS
AND WET MYSELF WHILE THEY ALL POINT AND
LAUGH!

FLASH ENTERS, SURROUNDED BY GIRLS.

PETER
Flash? Peter Parker. I just need a quote for the yearbook.

FLASH
WHO, PETER WHO?
LOOK NERD, I DON'T HAVE TIME FOR YOU.
YOU WANNA TALK TO ME?
NICE TRY, BUT YOU'RE NOT THAT COOL!
WHO, PETER WHO?
THERE'S OTHER STUFF I GOTTA DO;
LIKE ANYTHING BUT SITTING HERE AND
WASTING TIME ON YOU!

STUDENTS
OH GOD! THE MID-TERMS START TOMORROW!
OH GOD! I'M RIPPING OUT MY HAIR!

GUYS
I'D RATHER GIVE MY MOM MY CELL PHONE-

SOME JERK
AND LET HER SWIPE THROUGH PICTURES
UNPREPARED.

KAREN
You better have something.

KATIE
YOU! PETER, YOU!
WE'RE GONNA CHOKE YOU TILL YOU'RE BLUE
PETER, BLUE!

KAREN
Did you get that quote?

PETER
No.

KATIE	KAREN
GREAT!	WHAT ARE WE
WHAT ARE WE	SUPPOSED TO DO?!
SUPPOSED TO DO?	

KATIE
YOU! PETER, YOU!
NOW GWEN STACEY IS IN THE QUEUE...

KAREN
Last chance, Peter!

KATIE & KAREN
SO TOUGHEN UP AND GET THAT QUOTE,
OR DON'T COME BACK,
YOUR YEARBOOK JOB IS THROUGH!

The students all freeze in place except for
PETER, as the stage is bathed in a blue wash.

PETER
IT HAPPENS JUST LIKE THAT...
EVERY TIME I TRY TO HAVE MY SAY
THEY TEAR ME DOWN, AND LOCK ME OUT, AND
PUSH ME RIGHT AWAY.
IT'S ALWAYS JUST LIKE THAT...

5

PETER (Cont)
AND IT'S BEEN SINCE FRESHMAN YEAR!
GOD, WHAT AM I DOING, WHAT AM I DOING?
GOD, WHAT AM I DOING HERE?!

Lights up to full as the students freak out.

STUDENTS
OH GOD! THE MID-TERMS START TOMORROW!
I'M FREAKING OUT, I'M SO BEHIND!
I'LL GET SOME ADDERALL FOR NEXT YEAR,
CAUSE A-D-D PLUS PRESSURE TIMES MY
PARENTS
EQUALS ME, LOSING MY MIND!
OH GOD!

> *The song ends in a flurry of note-cards which
> Gwen tossed in the air.*
>
> *The BELL RINGS. Students scatter like roaches,
> exiting.*
>
> *Gwen and Peter are left on stage alone picking
> up the note-cards.*

GWEN
Peter Parker. (Pause) Peter Parker?!

PETER
Me?

GWEN
Is there another Peter Parker in this school?

PETER
Oh... You know my name.

GWEN

Duh, you sit behind me in chemistry.

PETER

And History and Calculus!

GWEN

Um... yeah. Remember, Friday I bor-

PETER

Borrowed my iodine in lab! I wrote about it in my diary! I
mean, Oh... I... didn't realize that was you.

GWEN

Maybe you'd remember me if I blew bubbles with the cancer
cells?

PETER

That's dangerous!

GWEN

That's a joke.

PETER

Because Iodine stain turns cancer cells bright pink under a
microscope... that's the smartest joke I've heard in my life.

GWEN

Thanks. So, I've got one!

PETER

Me too!

| **PETER** | **GWEN** |
| What? | What? |

GWEN

I have a quote, for the year book?

PETER

Oh, right!

GWEN

That's what you were looking for, right?

PETER

Yes, definitely! Go ahead.

GWEN

"In life you don't lose, without gaining something too."

PETER

That's great!

GWEN

Ask me how I thought of it!

PETER

Um, OK! How did you-

Flash enters.

SONG 04. "HURRICANE FLASH"

FLASH
(speak/singing)
GWEN STACY!
(musical sting)
I'M NOTICING MAYBE
(musical sting)
THE NERDY GIRL'S TURNED INTO A HOTTIE

GWEN
(breathy)
Flash Thompson knows my name?

FLASH
YOUR TUMMY GOT FLAT
OOH, HOW BOUT THAT
MAYBE SOMEONE'S BEEN DOING PILATES?

GWEN
Actually, I have! Every week! Thanks for noticing!

FLASH
I have a good eye, I'm a noticer... I'd be great as a crime
scene witness. People say that about me.

GWEN
Flash, you know Peter Parker?

FLASH
PETER, WHO?
DO I KNOW YOU?
WHATEVER KID, NICE TO MEET ME

ANYWAY, LET'S HAVE A DATE
WE CAN STUDY GOOD AND LATE
LEARNING AND FEELIN' OUR CHEMISTRY

Gwen, mid-terms, whoooh, people are tense, not me, I drink
green tea. Not all the time, but enough to say I drink it.

GWEN
Oh!

FLASH
YOU'RE CAUGHT IN THE EYE OF HURRICANE
FLASH
BETTER LEAVE THE POOL IF YOUR FACE DON'T
WANT MY SPLASH
I'M MOVING DOWN YOUR BODY LIKE AN UN-
CURABLE RASH
OH, OH, OH, OH, FLASH!
THOMPSON!

GWEN
(a little smitten)
Oh my god! You remind me of what my mom loved about
my dad before he left!

PETER
So where DID that quote come from?

FLASH
Who are you? Whatever.

GWEN, YOU AND ME ALONE
THE "R" TRAIN DOWN-TOWN
WE'LL HAVE A STUDY DATE TOMORROW
ONE LITTLE THING MORE
I LOST MY METRO CARD
SO BRING AN EXTRA 'MONTHLY' I CAN
BORROW?

GWEN
Um, wow, ok. I guess I'll see you then.

FLASH
YOU'RE CAUGHT IN THE EYE OF HURRICANE
FLASH
I'M LIKE A SEXY MEADOW WHERE YOU SPREAD
YOUR GRANDMA'S ASH
I'LL MAKE YOU FEEL AMAZING LIKE WHEN AL
GORE RECYCLES TRASH
OH, OH, OH, OH, FLASH!
THOMPSON!

Flash! Thompson...

> *Flash exits.*

PETER

Gwen?

GWEN
(lost in thought)
GREEN TEA!
(back)
Peter, sorry... was I saying something? I lost my thought.

PETER
That's OK, I got your quote.

GWEN
Great! Talk to you soon Peter Parker!

> *Gwen exits, the lights soften and isolate Peter.*

<u>SONG 04A. "PETER, WHO? (REPRISE 1)"</u>

PETER
WHO, PETER WHO?
I DON'T KNOW WHAT I HAVE TO DO
TO FIN'LY STICK OUT FROM THE CROWD,
AND MAKE A FRIEND OR TWO...
WHO, PETER WHO?

BLACKOUT.

SCENE 2

INT. AUNT MAY'S HOUSE, LIVING ROOM - EVENING

Comic-panel looks like the living room of a suburban house.

AUNT MAY is at a table folding laundry. There is a basket of clothes next to her.

PETER is there helping. He's mangling laundry, his fury causes more damage than help.

PETER
(Angrily, to himself)
...lost your stupid monthly metro card! Hope you choke on that green tea!

AUNT MAY
Peter! Stop it! You're mangling your big-boy underpants!

PETER
Sorry, Aunt May.

AUNT MAY
Come here...
(feels head)
You look sweaty. You don't have a fever, do you?

PETER
No.

AUNT MAY
The first symptom of bird-flu is a fever.

PETER

I don't have bird-flu, Aunt May.

AUNT MAY

That's what you said four years ago, but remember what happened?

PETER

I got bird-flu.

AUNT MAY

You got bird-flu! It's still a thing, you know? Just because it's not the trendy pandemic anymore doesn't mean it just vanished. It's still a big problem in China.

PETER

I don't have bird-flu, Aunt May! There's a girl... at school--

Aunt May begins hyperventilating casually.

PETER

And I really like her--

Aunt May is huffing harder...

PETER

I always thought the best way to like someone was quietly and from a safe distance, but she was talking to me, like on purpose and--

Aunt May is in a breathy frenzy!

AUNT MAY

See! I told you!

PETER

Aunt May, calm down... breathe! Breathe slowly.

AUNT MAY

(Trying to reign it in)

I told you eventually someone would see all the great things you offer!

PETER

Well, that's the thing...

AUNT MAY

Should I have your uncle talk to you? You know... about... reproduction?

PETER

No, Aunt May!

AUNT MAY

Because he's very comfortable to talk to... about... Reproduction.

PETER

I get it, Aunt May.

AUNT MAY

And he knows... REPRODUCTION!

PETER

No, Aunt May! Stop! Besides... Before I could say much, Flash Thompson came in, and in less than a minute she has a date with HIM this weekend.

AUNT MAY

Oh, Peter... I'm sorry dear.

PETER

He doesn't even try and he gets everything!

AUNT MAY

Well maybe so he's better at being 'cool', what are you better at? Where do you shine, sweetie?

PETER

I don't know... I'm good at photography... I like taking pictures, I guess...

AUNT MAY

Well, focus on that, focus on what you're good at and she'll notice.

PETER

It doesn't matter, not when guys like Flash exist. He's a total jerk, he cheats on all his tests but made honor roll cause our football team won state last year...

AUNT MAY

There are always going to be people like that in your life. Some people have to put a lot of effort into getting a little, and some people get to put little effort into getting a lot. Welcome to the lower middle-class.

SONG 05. "NICE GUYS"

PETER

WHAT ABOUT WORKING HARD, AND CARING?
WHAT ABOUT DOING WHAT YOU'RE TOLD?
I TRY TO GET NOTICED FOR THE GOOD THINGS I DO
BUT LOSING IS GETTING OLD
I JUST WANT TO BE ACKNOWLEDGED

PETER (Cont)
FOR THE THINGS THAT THEY CAN'T SEE
WHEN WILL THEY FIN'LY NOTICE ME?

AUNT MAY

Oh, Peter...

MAYBE YOU'RE SAD CAUSE FLASH IS
HANDSOME
WITH HIS JAW A PERFECT SQUARE
AND BAD BOYS ALWAYS GET THE GIRL
WITH A FLICK OF THEIR FLOWING HAIR
GIRLS YOUR AGE ARE SHORT-SIGHTED
DON'T SEE THE FOREST FOR THE WOOD
THEY'D RATHER HAVE A HANDSOME MAN
THEN A MAN WHO'S ANY GOOD

PETER

Thanks, Aunt May.

AUNT MAY

I'm bad at expressions, but...

NICE GUYS FINISH FIRST
BEING GANGLY IS NO DETERRENT
WHEN A GIRL IS READY TO MARRY
SHE DOESN'T CARE HOW COOL YOU'RE
WEREN'T!
NICE GUYS FINISH FIRST
THESE BAD TIMES WILL PASS IN JUST A BLINK
AND NICE GUYS FINISH FIRST... I THINK!
MAYBE YOU'RE JEALOUS CAUSE INSTEAD OF
THE PROM
YOU'LL SIT HOME ALONE AND READ
WHILE FLASH IS VOTED PROM KING
AND MOST LIKELY TO SUCCEED

AUNT MAY (CONT)
IT'S THE SQUEAKY WHEEL THAT GETS THE
GREASE
AND GET IT RUBBED UNDER THEIR HOOD
BUT EVENTUALLY THAT GREASE DRIES UP
AND GUYS LIKE YOU START LOOKING GOOD.

PETER

OK, Aunt May...

AUNT MAY
CUZ NICE GUYS FINISH FIRST
THOUGH YOU MAYBE CAN'T SEE HOW
THEY SAY LIFE BEGINS AT THIRTY

Do they say that?

SO, YOU'RE STILL IN PREVIEWS NOW
NICE GUYS FINISH FIRST
SO, PICK YOUR HEART UP OFF THE FLOOR
BECAUSE NICE GUYS FINISH FIRST... I'M PRETTY
SURE!

PETER	AUNT MAY
YOU SAY ONE DAY	
IT WILL BE FUN,	
WELL	
I SEE NO LIGHT	
AT THE END OF THIS	
TUNNEL	
WHEN WILL	SEE YOUR GAME IS
SOMEBODY EVER	THE LONG GAME
NOTICE ME?	THOUGH YOU WANT
I JUST WANT THEM	IT ALL SO FAST
TO START TO	BY THE TIME
NOTICE ME?	YOU'RE MY AGE,
WHEN WILL	GUYS LIKE
SOMEBODY EVER	FLASH END UP
NOTICE ME?	PUMPING YOUR GAS
I JUST WANT THEM	
TO START TO	
NOTICE ME?	
WHEN WILL	
SOMEBODY EVER	
NOTICE ME?	
ETC...	

A chorus of people enter, dressed as yard-workers. They dance with Aunt May.

AUNT MAY & ENSEMBLE
NICE GUYS FINISH FIRST
AND YOU'LL SMILE WITH YOUR LAST BREATH
BECAUSE CHILDHOOD IS SUCH A SMALL PART
OF THE RACE
WHEN THE FINISH LINE IS DEATH
YOU MAY NOT GET TO PARTY WITH POST
MALONE

AUNT MAY & ENSEMBLE(CONT)
YOU'RE BORING NOW, WAIT TILL YOU'RE
GROWN!
CAUSE NICE GUYS FINISH FIRST
YOU'LL NEVER GET ARRESTED AT BONAROO,
LOSE A BET AND GET A NECK TATTOO
CAUSE NICE GUYS FINISH FIRST
OLDER WOMEN NEED A SOLID SHOULDER
AND BEAUTY IS IN THE EYE OF THE BEHOLDER
CAUSE NICE GUYS FINISH FIRST
THEY LAUGHED CAUSE YOU WERE NO CLARK
GABLE
YOU'LL LAUGH WHEN THEY NEED A MAN
WHO'S STABLE
CAUSE NICE GUYS FINISH FIRST
JUST WAIT AND YOU WILL SEE!
NICE GUYS FINISH FIRST
EVENTUALLY!

PETER
Who are all these people and what are they doing in our
house?!

AUNT MAY
Oh, it's just the yard-workers.

MAN
The back yard is tidy, miss. Let's go round front to trim that
bush.

AUNT MAY
Thanks boys and Trish! Peter, if you want her to notice you,
focus on what makes you special!

SONG 05A. "Scene Change NICE GUYS"

*INT. OFFICES OF THE 'DAILY BUGLE' -
MORNING*

*The newspaper office: The Daily Bugle; The
comic-panel background depicts desks and
reporters with a window that reads 'Daily
Bugle.'*

*BETTY is sitting at her desk upstage center; she
is focused on her Sudoku book.*

PETER enters.

PETER
Hi, I'm Peter Parker, I saw online that you offer internships
for students--

BETTY
Peter who?

PETER
Parker.

BETTY
Do you have an appointment?

PETER
No. I wanted to ask about your internships--

BETTY
Ohh, we're pretty full right now.
            (looking up)
Wow, your face is really symmetrical. Do people tell you
that? They probably don't but not because it's not true! I'm

BETTY (CONT)

Betty, Betty Brant. This is my desk. Usually there are flowers, but I've been cleaning. Welcome to the Daily Bugle.

PETER

Thanks!

JAMESON (OFFSTAGE)

BETTY!!!
> (he enters)

I have two jobs for you - one is staying on top of my photographers, riding 'em to meet their deadlines. The other is brewing coffee. Now, I know that coffee comes more naturally to you.

BETTY

The directions are so clear!

JAMESON

And you make a hell of a cup. But I was just on the phone with Ditko and he's hysterical! Crying to me that he doesn't have a photographer to help him cover this Blatant Science Expo tomorrow! Now I hate a lot of things in this world, Brant... even some things that it's not trendy to hate - like recycling programs! But nothing, nothing so much as grown men who cry.

BETTY

It's not my fault JJ. I had Simonson on it, but he fell down a flight of stairs in his apartment building yesterday, he was coming home with groceries, I don't know details but there were two gallons of milk. Gallons are heavy JJ. Anyway, he's in bad shape.

JAMESON

Betty, when was the last time you heard a middle-aged man cry?

BETTY

I don't know.

> *JAMESON crosses to BETTY'S desk and presses a button on her phone.*

DITKO (OFFSTAGE)
(sobbing hysterically)
Please... Jonah, for science... I'm so emotional!

> *Jameson hits a button to turn the speaker off.*

JAMESON

Disgusting, isn't it?

BETTY

What about Helix?

JAMESON

Helix is already on assignment. Covering that soviet master-of-disguise run amok... Chameleon or something... great name, wish I thought of it! Page one material. Something about mind-control. Who else?

PETER

I'll do it!

JAMESON

Shut up! Who are you? Who is this?

BETTY

JJ, meet Peter Parker. Great photographer!

JAMESON

Parker, eh?

(he looks Peter over)

You a crier?

PETER

Um, no sir.

> *Jameson grabs Peter's hand and puts his cigar out in Peter's palm, watching eagerly as Peter silently shrieks.*

JAMESON

Just had to make sure. This interview is over go bring me some stellar photos, otherwise don't bother coming back at all.

> *Jameson exits.*

PETER

Hey, thank you!

BETTY

No problem, maybe soon you'll know me well enough to compliment me too. Not that I'm high maintenance... I'm really not. I'm like a Honda civic... turn me on once and I'm good for years!

PETER

Ok.

BETTY

First in class in comfort and reliability.

PETER

Cool.

BETTY

2018 Motor-Trend car of the year--

PETER

I should really get going!

BETTY

Don't let me stop you.

SONG 05B. "Scene Change HERO"

SCENE 4

EXT. SUBWAY PLATFORM - AFTERNOON

The comic-panel is one of an outdoor subway platform.

PETER is on stage with his camera and bag getting ready to head for the expo.

There is a MAN sitting on a bench looking oddly with a newspaper in his hand, he is 'The One' for the scene.

GWEN enters.

GWEN
Peter Parker!

PETER
Gwen, hey!

GWEN
Were you just working out? You're sweating pretty hard.

PETER
--yeah... pretty hard.

GWEN	PETER	MAN ON BENCH
What?	What?	What?

GWEN
Hey, cool camera!

PETER

Thanks, I'm going to the Science Expo, to take pictures for the Daily Bugle! I got an internship.

GWEN

You're going to the expo? That's great, I read about it.

PETER

Really?

GWEN

Yeah! I mean, cuz of mid-terms science is beyond stressing me right now, but I'm still into it!

PETER

Really, really? I'm awesome at it! If you ever wanted to maybe study-

Flash enters.

FLASH

I hope somebody's ready for zesty burritos.

GWEN

Flash, Peter and I were just talking about the Science Expo! He's taking pictures for the Bugle, isn't that cool?

FLASH

Awesome, you're primed on science... That's gonna make chemistry totally easy Gwen. It's study time.

PETER

Where are you going?

FLASH

WE are going to Chipotle, I always study at Chipotle!

GWEN
He does!

FLASH
Their food is fresh. I got us a table, they don't hold tables for just anybody. They know me there.

PETER
You know, I don't actually have to be at the Expo for another hour, and I'm really good at chemistry.

GWEN
Oh, that would be great, Peter!

FLASH
The table's for two. It's a pretty exclusive Chipotle.

Music starts.

SONG 06. "CHIPOTLE"

FLASH
THERE'S A TABLE AT CHIPOTLE
WAITING JUST FOR YOU AND ME
BY THE SALSA BAR, THE SALSA BAR
WHERE WE BOTH CAN STUDY CHEMISTRY
I'LL LEAN OVER, AS WE STUDY
MOVING CLOSER WITH MY HIPS
AND I'LL KISS YOU THERE, I WON'T MISS YOU
THERE
AS I TAKE YOUR FACE AND PRESS IT TO MY
LIPS.
AT CHIPOTLE!

A CHORUS of backup dancers salsa on, holding
Chipotle bags filled with tortilla chips which
they use as maracas. They accentuate the
romance in Flash's head.

CHORUS
CHIPOTLE!

FLASH
I STUDY AT CHIPOTLE!

CHORUS
CHIPOTLE!

FLASH
AT CHIPOTLE!

CHORUS
CHIPOTLE!

FLASH
I REALLY STUDY AT CHIPOTLE!

ALL
CHI-POT-LE!

PETER
THE MID-TERM IS INTENSE THIS YEAR
IT'S JUST FIVE DAYS AWAY

GWEN
IT COULDN'T HURT TO HAVE HIS HELP
SO FLASH, WHAT DO YOU SAY?

FLASH
Parker, can I talk to you over here for a second?

Flash takes Peter off to the side, away from Gwen. As Flash sings his temper escalates.

FLASH
I AM FLASH
AND YOU'RE A NERD
LET ME HELP YOU FIND A CAB!
GO BACK HOME
AND TAKE YOUR BOOKS
OVER TO YOUR SCIENCE LAB!
AND IF YOU TRY TO STICK YOUR NOSE
WHERE I THINK IT DON'T BELONG
IT MIGHT BREAK BENEATH MY FIST
CAUSE I'M DEF'NITLY THAT STRONG!

PETER
Gwen, I think-

FLASH
DON'T IGNORE ME
DON'T YOU START
CAUSE I'LL FINISH THIS TONIGHT
HOLD MY SHIRT
I'VE GOT THIS GUY
HOPE YOU'RE READY FOR A FIGHT!

GWEN
Flash, no!

FLASH
CAN'T YOU HEAR HIM BEGGIN' ME
TO ERASE HIS PUNY FACE?!

GWEN
Peter, go!

PETER

I'm going.

FLASH

NOT SO FAST
MY KNUCKLES ITCH!

> *As the song escalates, and Flash is going to fight
> Peter; Gwen, in a last act of heroism, grabs
> Flash and kisses him to occupy him so Peter can
> escape.*

> *Peter does so, but not before seeing Gwen kiss
> Flash.*

GWEN

FLASH! NOT IN OUR PLACE...
AT CHIPOTLE!

CHORUS

AT CHIPOTLE!
WE STUDY IN CHIPOTLE!
ETC.
CHI-POT-LE!

> *They strike a final pose.*

SONG 06A. "Scene Change CHIPOTLE"

BLACKOUT.

SCENE 5

INT. SCIENCE LABORATORY - LATER IN THE AFTERNOON

The comic-panels are of a Science Lab, crazy instruments and spiders in test jars.

There is an old microwave prominently featured.

DR SPIDERMAN is there, PETER enters flanked by security guards, DR SPIDERMAN growls at the guards and motions them away, they exit confused and scared.

SPIDERMAN

Gahh! Forgive the extra security, apparently Russian spies are after my secrets... It's to be expected when you're a super genius. I'm Dr. Spiderman.

PETER

Spiderman?

SPIDERMAN

Spiddermin.

PETER

Spiddermin?

SPIDERMAN

Dr. Kurt Spiderman, two "D's", world famous Neuroscientist! Please, look around. My two big projects are: a very controversial and untested cure for lupus, and of course my highly coveted mind-control device!

PETER
(impressed)

Oh!

SPIDERMAN
(humbled)

Oh!

PETER
(excited)

Oh!

SPIDERMAN
(agreeing)

Oh!

PETER
(curious)

Oh!

SPIDERMAN

Oh, you see, I've figured out how to harness the power of the synapses in ways unimaginable to average society- Don't touch that!

> *PETER has been taking pictures of the instruments, and has found the old microwave.*

PETER

What is it?

SPIDERMAN

My microwave. It's crazy old, gives off terrible radiation and I've been making Hot Pockets in there all day.

PETER

Isn't that dangerous?

SPIDERMAN

Well, LEAN pockets.

PETER

No, the radiation! Isn't it dangerous?

SPIDERMAN

Not for me boy, I leave the room, but terrible for the spiders in those test jars.

PETER

Yeah, some of them look dead.

SPIDERMAN

Good. Trust me, better for us they're dead, if any of these spiders got loose who knows what they'd do to us! There was an independent study in Guatemala about radiation and spider venom... Now, I didn't read it... but there was a study!

> *A JANITOR enters with a broom, sweeping their way across the stage during SPIDERMAN'S speech.*

> *The JANITOR is 'The One' for the scene.*

SPIDERMAN

Now, don't tell the Russians I told you, but the brain is like a tesla coil and wireless router rolled into one, and you can tap into-

> *During Dr. Spiderman's speech, Peter starts itching, there is something crawling on him.*

Finally he slaps his neck!

PETER

Ow! My neck!

SPIDERMAN

What's wrong? Is it Lupus? I can fix it, maybe.

> *Dr. Spiderman pulls a large syringe out of his
> pocket.*

PETER

No, I think I was bit by something... hey, are all those spiders
accounted for?

SPIDERMAN

Look, I tightened those jars myself! Now come get this
doorknob for me, my wrists don't really turn anymore...
> (as he exits)
Look at that, it's a PUSH door... I don't need help after all...
Should have tried that days ago--

> *Lights swirl a little.*

> *Dr. Spiderman exits, but Peter is feeling queasy.*

> *Music starts.*

SONG 07. "A NEW PETER PARKER"

PETER
I FEEL STRANGE
SOMETHING'S CHANGIN' INSIDE OF ME
REARRANGIN' AT A MIND-BLOWIN' RATE
SHOULD BE SCARED

COULD BE CANCER, KNOWIN' MY LUCK
WASN'T PREPARED FOR CANCER TO FEEL THIS...
GREAT!

Peter jumps out of the window.

*The scene panels behind Peter change from the
bedroom to a city street, lined with cars, one of
which is a cardboard Prius. He walks along as
he continues to sing.*

THERE'S A POWER THAT'S SURGING INSIDE OF
ME
I'M FEELING STRONGER THAN EVER BEFORE
ALL THE WEAKNESS IS PURGING INSIDE OF ME

WHAT ELSE COULD LIFE HAVE IN STORE? OH!
I'M FINALLY FINISHED WITH ALL OF THE
LABELS I'VE WORN
IT'S A NEW START, A NEW DAY, A NEW LIFE, A
NEW WAY
SO THANKS OLD MICROWAVE
A NEW PETER PARKER IS BORN!
I AM FEELING SO STRONG I COULD PICK UP A
PRIUS
AND HOIST IT RIGHT OVER MY HEAD.
WHAT THE HELL, THERE'S A PRIUS IN FRONT OF
ME
AWESOME! I'M LIFTING IT AND I'M NOT DEAD.

*He grabs the cardboard Prius and lifts it above
his head. Then he throws it off-stage and a loud
explosion is heard.*

PETER (CONT)
WHILE THE SUN'S IN THE SKY
I CAN JUMP AND SAY 'HI' TO THE DAWN

Peter takes his glasses, and throws them offstage, another explosion is heard.

LOOK UP THERE AND YOU'LL SEE ME
A POWERFUL FREE ME
IT SUCKS NOT TO BE ME
A NEW PETER PARKER IS BORN!

INT. AUNT MAY'S HOUSE - PETER'S BEDROOM

Three ensemble members enter carrying cardboard cutouts of Peter's room he crawls across his walls and cieling.

I CAN FLY AND WALK ON WALLS
SUDDENLY ADVENTURE CALLS
IT'S A NEW LIFE FOR
ME TO ENJOY IT IS WHAT I HAVE SWORN
FROM NOW ON I'M UNFETTERED
I'LL BE A TREND-SETTER
LIFE JUST GOT MUCH BETTER
A NEW PETER PARKER IS BORN!

A FEW DAYS LATER.

SCENE 6

INT. PETER'S BEDROOM - DAY

Half the stage is in darkness where Uncle Ben sits frozen. The half that is lit has a comic-panel of a bedroom.

PETER wakes up in a panic, spandex stuck to his hands. He shakes it frantically trying to get it off.

PETER
(trying to shake the spandex off his hand)
Hey... Get off! Come on... Off! Get off!

AUNT MAY enters.

AUNT MAY
What's going on Peter, why are you screaming?

PETER
(Shaking a piece of blue and red spandex)
...I can't... get off!

AUNT MAY
Calm down!

PETER
Aunt May!

AUNT MAY

Peter, my friends are over for Mahjong, and all we hear is you screaming! What are you doing to your old gymnastics costume?

>*Aunt May's 2 FRIENDS peek their head in the door.*

FRIEND 1

It sounds like a bad time, we're just gonna go.

FRIEND 2

We'll see you Sunday though.

FRIEND 1

Yeah, bye.

FRIEND 2

Bye Peter.

>*They exit.*

AUNT MAY

There Peter! You ruined Mahjong! Is that what you wanted? Because that's what happened!

PETER

I wasn't trying to ruin Mahjong... I just... nothing.

AUNT MAY

Peter, where did your glasses go?

PETER

I don't need them anymore.

AUNT MAY

Puberty doesn't do that, Peter! Remember what happened
last time you didn't wear your glasses?

PETER

I walked into a man-hole.

AUNT MAY

You walked right into a man-hole! We had to call the fire
department to get you out. Here, take your prescription swim
goggles.

PETER

I don't need them!

AUNT MAY

It's not a discussion, Peter! I'm not fishing you out of the
sewer today. What's going on? This isn't like you. You're so
moody these last few days. And, I wasn't going to say
anything but what's all that gunk I keep cleaning off your
walls?

PETER
(in wonder)
Aunt May, it's from my hands!

AUNT MAY

That's what I was afraid of.

PETER

Like OUT OF my hands, I mean, like a spider or something!

AUNT MAY

You're gonna go blind, Peter! You HAVE to talk to your
Uncle. I can't keep going in circles like this.

PETER

You know what, fine!

AUNT MAY

Good! Thank you! And you look chilly, take your red hoodie, you don't wanna catch the bird-flu.

PETER

Thanks.

> *MAY holds out his red hoodie and PETER takes it and crosses to the other side of the stage.*

SONG 07A. "Scene Change TO UNCLE BEN"

> *LIGHTS CROSS-FADE.*

SCENE 7

INT. THE KITCHEN - CONTINUOUS

UNCLE BEN is sitting at the kitchen table paying bills.

PETER enters from the other side of the stage.

PETER
Uncle Ben, do you have a minute?

UNCLE BEN
Sure Peter, just finishing bills. You're too young to have to worry, but responsibility as a man always seems to be staggeringly financial. What's on your mind?

PETER
Uncle Ben... I don't know... I've... something's kind of different. Like inside me. There are changes in my body, that I don't understand...

UNCLE BEN
Oh god... Oh Peter...

PETER
I'm going crazy, I'm sorry.

UNCLE BEN
No! No, it's fine. I'm ready for this... I've spent two years at crafting workshops preparing for just this occasion.

PETER
Uncle Ben--

UNCLE BEN

Don't stop me, Peter. Once I get going, I rely on momentum...

Uncle Ben takes two hand puppets, a male and female, off the bookshelf and puts them on.

UNCLE BEN (AS MALE PUPPET)

Excuse me miss, you look fertile and of an age to settle down.

UNCLE BEN (AS FEMALE PUPPET)

And you look like your credit score is at least seven-hundred.

UNCLE BEN (AS MALE PUPPET)

Seven-sixty since I paid off my student loans.

UNCLE BEN (AS FEMALE PUPPET)

You paid off your student loans? Like in full?! Take me now!

PETER

Uncle Ben! Stop!   This isn't about... Reproduction!

UNCLE BEN

Whew! I think I sweated through my shirt.

PETER

Me too. I mean... well, there's a guy that no one respects or appreciates, but I think there's a real hero inside him that's just been hard to see before.

UNCLE BEN

Peter, I can't tell you how great it is to hear you say that. It makes everything worth it.

PETER

Really?

Music starts.

SONG 08. "HERO OF MEN"

UNCLE BEN

I AM A HERO!
A HERO OF MEN!
IT'S GREAT TO HEAR YOU SAY IT, PETER
AND I'LL SAY AGAIN!

PETER

No... I meant-

UNCLE BEN

I AM A HERO
A HERO OF MEN
I'M SUPER DEADLY WITH A CHECKBOOK AND A
BALLPOINT PEN.
NO, I'VE NEVER MISSED A PAYMENT ON OUR
CABLE BILL, AMEN!
I AM A HERO
A HERO OF MEN
AND PETER THERE WILL COME A DAY
FOR YOU TO BE A HERO TOO
THOUGH YOU MAY NOT KNOW RIGHT NOW,
YOU'LL SEE.
THERE'S POWER IN BECOMING
WHAT YOU WILL SOON BECOME,
BUT WITH GREAT POWER COMES GREAT
RESPONSIBILITY!
I AM A HERO
A HERO OF MEN

UNCLE BEN (CONT)
PAYING DOWN A MORTGAGE IS MY SUPER-
STRENGTH
AND NAPPING IN THE DEN!
I AM A HERO
A HERO OF MEN
THE TRASH WILL NEVER SIT TOO LONG
MY NETFLIX CUE IS NEVER WRONG ON THIS IS
SWEAR,
AS SURE AS MY NAME IS BEN:
I'M A HERO OF MEN!

SONG 08A. "Scene Change HERO OF MEN"

BLACKOUT.

EXT. THE CITY STREETS - VARIOUS

Time has passed. The comic-panel is of a city street.

The stage is bathed in blue light, the townsfolk take the stage, they're all buried in their newspapers, which sport headlines about a 'Human Spider.'

SONG 09. "WHO IS THE MAN?"

TOWNSPEOPLE
DID YOU READ ABOUT THE MAN
WHO THEY SAW CLIMBING UP A BUILDING?

SOLO
DID YOU READ ABOUT THE MAN
WHO LEAPS TO ROOFS FROM FAR BELOW?

TWO
DID YOU READ ABOUT THE MAN
WHO'S TRUE IDENTITY IS SECRET?

TOWNSPEOPLE
TELL ME WHERE HE COMES FROM,
TELL ME NOW CAUSE I NEED TO KNOW!
WHO IS THE MAN?
WHO IS THE MAN, WHO IS AGILE LIKE A
SPIDER?
WHO IS THE MAN?
WHO IS THE MAN, THAT MYSTERIOUS
OUTSIDER?

SOLO
I THINK I SAW HIM ON A BUILDING
NEAR THE CORNER OF COLUMBUS AND
EIGHTY-THIRD.

TWO
I SAW HIM SWINGING THROUGH THE CITY
TAKING SELFIES ON HIS PHONE.

A FEW
HE WAS A VISION FOR AN INSTANT
IN THE SHADOWS OF THE EVENING, OR SO I'VE
HEARD.

TOWNSPEOPLE
AND WHEN I SEE HIM IN THE NEWS
HE'S LIKE A GUY I FEEL I KNOW

> *A camera flashes and Peter is standing with his
> back to the audience wearing a red hoodie with
> a white spider painted on the back, and a red
> mask.*

> *After he stages another photo he changes out of
> his costume back to his street clothes.*

PETER
THINGS ARE CHANGING FOR PETER PARKER
NO MORE LIVING WITH SUCH CONCERN
MAKING MONEY BY STAGING THESE
PHOTOGRAPHS
MAKES IT MY TURN, MY TURN.

> *TRANSITION TO:*
> *INT. 'DAILY BUGLE' OFFICE - VARIOUS*

The townsfolk freeze in a tableau as the light on them fades down, lights come up on Betty at her desk at the Bugle. Peter returns to deliver his photos.

BETTY

Peter, I got these flowers, the card says they're from you. How did you know I keep flowers on my desk?

PETER

That's your handwriting, Betty.

BETTY
(Whispering)
There's chemistry between us. It's so palpable I can smell it... we reek of it!

Jameson enters.

JAMESON

Peter, stop flirting with Betty, no work-place romance! What, you think I'm heartless? Damn right I am, or will be! I'm an organ donor! Parker, are those more photos? They're terrible, but I'll use 'em, pay him half.

> *JAMESON hands PETER a wad of money, they exit, BETTY freezes at her desk. Time elapses, and the lights cross-fade back to the townsfolk in the city streets, who are again pouring over newspapers.*

> *EXT. THE CITY STREETS - NIGHT*

SOLO
DID YOU READ ABOUT THE SPIDER-MAN,
THE CHAMPION OF WRESTLERS?

TWO
DID YOU READ ABOUT THE SPIDER-MAN?
HE'S PUTTING ON A SHOW.

A FEW
DID YOU READ ABOUT THE SPIDER-MAN,
WHO LIFTED UP A PRIUS?

TOWNSPEOPLE
TELL ME WHERE HE COMES FROM,
TELL ME NOW CAUSE I NEED TO KNOW!
WHO IS THE MAN?
WHO IS THE MAN, WHO IS SWINGING THROUGH
OUR CITY?
WHO IS THE MAN?
WHO IS THE MAN, WHOSE PECKS POP LIKE
THEY'RE IN 3-D?

SOLO
THE DAILY BUGLE SHOWED HIM SWINGING BY
THE APPLE STORE
SO I BOUGHT AN APPLE WATCH!

TWO
IT TELLS THE TIME AND TAKES MY HEART BEAT
WHEN I'M GOING FOR A RUUUUN!

GUY DOING STEROIDS
I HEARD THAT SPIDER-MAN CAN DEAD-LIFT
MORE THAN ME
SO NOW I'M KICKING IT UP A NOTCH!

TOWNSPEOPLE
I DON'T KNOW WHY HE'S IN THE NEWS,
BUT THIS GUY IS SUPER FUN!!

*Again, the camera flashes and Peter, dressed in
his Spider-Man mask/hoodie steps out, and
changes back into his street clothes. He tucks his
costume into his camera bag.*

PETER
THINGS ARE CHANGING FOR PETER PARKER
UNCLE BEN, I HAVE REALLY LEARNED.
I'VE GOT MONEY AND FAME, ALL THAT I COULD
WANT
NOW IT'S MY TURN, FIN'LY MY TURN.

*The townsfolk freeze in a tableau as the light on
them fades down, lights come up on Betty at her
desk at the Bugle. Peter returns to deliver his
photos.*

INT. DAILY BUGLE - CONTINUOUS

BETTY
Peter, do you like my new glasses?

PETER
They're great Betty.

BETTY
This is a picture I drew of a lighthouse, that I want to buy
with you in northern Maine... you know, when we're ready
to settle down.

Jameson enters.

JAMESON
Peter, you're freelance. Keep bringing me pictures, but I'm
not paying you extra! What, do you need the money?
Gambling problem? You're taking risks kid. You think I

JAMESON (CONT)
took risks? Damn right I did. Real risks, I played the Russians in Roulette... turns out their rules are different, but I'm not about to let Putin scare me off! Fine, I'll use these, pay him half.

JAMESON hands PETER another wad of cash, they exit, BETTY freezes at her desk.

EXT. THE CITY STREETS - NIGHT

Time elapses and the lights cross-fade, the townsfolk are reading more newspapers.

PETER is taking pictures of himself as Spider-Man and then finishes, a BANK ALARM is heard. This is THE robbery.

PERSON
Spider-man! Help that bank is being robbed! Anyone paying a mortgage might be in real trouble!

PETER
Sorry, I gotta get these pictures back! Good luck.

Peter sheds his costume and is surrounded by the townsfolk as they circle him with papers singing.

TOWNSPEOPLE	PETER
WHO IS THE MAN?	THINGS ARE
WHO IS THE MAN?	CHANGING
ETC...	THINGS ARE
	CHANGING
	ETC...

The music swells to a climax but before it resolves it is cut off by Betty, the lights immediately fade back to the Bugle setting, and the townsfolk silently exit in darkness.

Betty hands the phone to Peter. Standing off on the other side of the stage in spot-light is Doctor Brenner.

INT. DAILY BUGLE - CONTINUOUS

BETTY

Peter, there's a phone call for you.

PETER

Hello?

DOCTOR
(On the phone)

Is this Peter Parker?

PETER

Yes.

DOCTOR

This is Doctor Brenner, at the hospital, you'd better come quick son, there's been an incident with your uncle.

PETER

Which hospital?

DOCTOR

Ah, right! New York Presbyterian, on Lexington!

PETER

I'll be right over, 4th and Lexington...

DOCTOR

Ah, no, that's the downtown hospital, we're on 23rd and Lexington.

PETER

OK, near Madison Square Park! Got it.

DOCTOR

Ah, no again, 23rd AVENUE and Lexington STREET, in Queens, Peter.

PETER

Is that the one by the Greek Diner?

DOCTOR

It WAS an Greek Diner, now it's an Arbies!

PETER

On my way!

DOCTOR

WAIT! We're not near the Arbies! That's a different hospital entirely!

PETER

WHERE ARE YOU?!?!

DOCTOR

Across the street! 44-81 23rd Avenue. It's the big hospital-shaped building!

PETER

I'll be right there!

DOCTOR

Please, hurry.

INT. HOSPITAL WAITING ROOM - NIGHT

The comic-panel shows a hospital waiting room.

*PETER is pacing the floor, after a moment the
DOCTOR enters.*

DOCTOR

Are you Peter?

PETER

Yes.

DOCTOR

Oh good, we'll just wait for your Aunt May so I can give you
both the terrible news while you're together.

PETER

Terrible news? How's Uncle Ben?

DOCTOR

I'd really prefer wait. It's too scarring to listen to twice.

PETER

What? What happened? Where is he?

DOCTOR

Oh, you are prodding me... but trust me you'll want a
shoulder to cry on when I discuss the gruesome details.

PETER

Is he... is he dead?

Aunt May enters, overhearing Peter's last line.

AUNT MAY

What? Ben is dead?

DOCTOR

Ah, good. Aunt May is here, now we can begin. Yes, Uncle Ben IS dead, I'm so sorry. The "official" cause of death is the gunshot from the bank robbery, but I insisted that I do a second autopsy myself. In the name of being thorough! I started at the head, you see aneurysms can often present as gunshot wounds, so I cut the head off at the neck to really get a good look in there...

AUNT MAY

Oh, Peter!

As the music swells the DOCTOR'S volume fades out, but he continues to mime talking, as a spotlight appears on PETER.

SONG 10. "WITH GREAT POWER"

PETER

LIKE ALL MY LIFE I'D BEEN LIVING UNDER
WATER
IN A SNAP, JUST LIKE THAT, I CAN SAY
GOODBYE TO ORDER
YOUR ADVICE, GREAT ADVICE, BUT I TOOK IT
FOR THE SURFACE
NOT YOU'RE GONE, ALL MY FAULT,
CAUSE I KNOW I COULD HAVE STOPPED IT
I SHOULD HAVE STOPPED IT!
BUT NO!
I DIDN'T THINK AT ALL I IGNORED THE CALL!
IT'S TOO LATE, BUT I UNDERSTAND
IT'S TOO LATE, BUT I FIN'LY SEE

PETER (CONT)
THAT WITH GREAT POWER
COMES GREAT RESPONSIBILITY

AUNT MAY enters and the DOCTOR goes to her
and continues explaining what happened to Ben.

DOCTOR
With the head yielding nothing new, I went into the legs!
Start from the ends and work inward! That's what my
mentor, Jeffrey Dahmer, used to say. Oh, not THAT Jeffrey
Dahmer, this man a genius, ahead of his time... ironically he
was killed by THAT Jeffrey Dahmer. So after dissolving the
legs thoroughly in acid, I realized I forgot to inspect them
before they were gone--

PETER
WHAT TO DO? WHERE TO GO?
EVERY SECOND FEELS A MINUTE
I'M ALONE, SENSE OF HOME
HAS VANISHED OUT THE WINDOW
ONE WRONG CHOICE, YOU'RE NOT THERE, IT
ONLY TOOK A MOMENT
IT ISN'T FAIR, NOTHING'S FAIR, HOW COULD I
LET IT HAPPEN
WHY DID I LET IT HAPPEN?
BUT NO!
I DIDN'T THINK AT ALL I IGNORED THE CALL!
NOW IT'S TOO LATE, I UNDERSTAND
IT'S TOO LATE, I FIN'LY SEE
THAT WITH GREAT POWER COMES GREAT
RESPONSIBILITY.

The DOCTOR fades up again, he is still talking
to MAY who is now convulsive with tears.

DOCTOR
With the appendages revealing nothing "Conclusive" it was time dispense the coyness. I dug into the chest cavity with fervor and a small axe. The lungs... pink and healthy aside from the odd hatchet-scrape, clearly of no use. The heart... sure there was a gunshot there... we all knew that going in. But the kidneys... well, those were fine too. Anyway, there's no body left to bury, I'm so sorry for your loss. Now if you'll just sign these papers--

Unable to handle the Doctor, PETER leaves the hospital to the streets outside, the lighting is darker, and Peter begins noticing a troubled city he had never seen before.

TRANSITION TO:

EXT. THE CITY STREETS - NIGHT

Maybe there's a garbage can on fire... you know, a city in trouble.

SOLO 1
SOMEBODY SAVE MY BABY!

SOLO 2
HELP, THIS BUILDING'S ON FIRE!

DUO
I THINK SOMEONE SHOT THE MAYOR!

OTHERS
THERE'S A BOMB ON THE BUS
THERE'S A BOMB ON THE BUS
THERE'S A BOMB ON THE BUS!

PETER
HOW COULD I HAVE BEEN SO BLIND
TO WHAT THIS CITY REALLY NEEDS?
LIKE I WAS CLOSING OFF MY MIND
TO THE CITY'S MIGHTY HEEDS!
I WILL SHOULDER THIS BURDEN AS LONG AS I
CAN
BE THE HERO I WAS MEANT TO BE.
I AM SPIDER-MAN!

TOWNSPEOPLE
IT'S TOO LATE

PETER
NOW I UNDERSTAND

TOWNSPEOPLE
IT'S TOO LATE

PETER
NOW I FINALLY SEE

ALL
THAT WITH GREAT POWER COMES
GREAT RESPONSIBILITY!

They freeze in their tableau.

BLACKOUT.

SCENE 10

INT. AUNT MAY'S LIVING ROOM - DAY

*In the far corner of the room is a coffee table
with a pile of lasagnas on it.*

*May is placing another lasagna on the pile,
wrought with grief. She slowly walks to Peter.*

*Peter is at a free-standing door, which is opened,
he waves off a visitor we don't see.*

*May's Friend walks to door, carrying another
lasagna, and rings the bell.*

FRIEND 1

Oh, Peter, dear. You look so skinny, I made you both a
lasagna, eat, I know it's hard right now.

*May reaches Peter, who hands her the new
lasagna.*

FRIEND 1

May, I'm so sorry dear, Ben was a great man. You'll never
find another one like him.

MAY
(Sobs)

*She turns around and slowly walks back to the
table.*

FRIEND 1

I wish I could stay, but Harry's in the car. It's date night.

She exits as Betty walks to the door, carrying a lasagna. She rings the bell.

BETTY

Peter, your cheeks look gaunt. I... I'm fairly domestic so I baked you a lasagna, it should be good, recipes.com gave it four stars.

Having dropped off the last dish, May reaches Peter, who hands her the new lasagna.

BETTY

Oh, May, I can't imagine what you're going through... they say you only have one true soul mate in the world.

MAY

(Sobs)

She turns around and slowly walks back to the table.

BETTY

Just to put this in your mind Peter, I always loved the name 'Ben' for my first son... or daughter.

PETER

Bye, Betty.

BETTY

I'm here when you need me.

Betty exits as Gwen enters, Lasagna in hand.

GWEN

Peter, I'm so sorry for your loss.

PETER

Gwen, hi.

GWEN

I figured you wouldn't want to cook so I made you a lasagna.

PETER

That's so thoughtful, thanks Gwen.

> *Having dropped off the last dish, May reaches Peter, who hands her the new lasagna.*

GWEN

My condolences May. I always admired your relationship with Ben... you guys made it. Like my parents never did.

MAY
(Sobs)

> *She turns around and slowly walks back to the table.*

GWEN

How are you? I've been thinking about you. If you ever-

> *A loud CAR HORN is heard from off.*

FLASH (OFFSTAGE)

Gwen!! Gwen?! I'm parking!

GWEN
(embarrassed)

Over here!

PETER

Things good with Flash?

GWEN

Well... the thing about Flash is-

Flash enters, carrying an empty lasagna tin.

FLASH

Gwen! There you are! Is this the kid?
(to Peter)
Sorry for your loss, kid. I didn't make you a lasagna--

GWEN

I told you--

FLASH

I PURCHASED one! I wouldn't show up empty handed,
Gwen.

GWEN

Where is it?

FLASH

I got hungry in the car.

GWEN

We're literally about to go to dinner!

FLASH

You're dating a furnace, Gwen. I need fuel to stay hot.

PETER

Well, thanks for stopping by, Gwen--

FLASH

My condolences, kid.

GWEN

Flash, you know Peter--

FLASH

Peter, who?

PETER

Parker!

FLASH

Oh, like that old guy who got shot last week.

Aunt May overhears, sobs, and exits.

GWEN

Oh God, I'm SO sorry, Peter! Flash, let's just go, OK?

FLASH

Hang on Gwen, listen kid, I didn't mean to be hard on ya. Truth is, I know what you're going through.

PETER

I doubt that.

Music starts

SONG 10A. "HURRICANE FLASH (REPRISE)"

FLASH
YOU'RE PRETTY SAD
SOMEONE KILLED YOUR DAD...

PETER
I mean, Uncle... but basically, yeah.

FLASH
THEY UP AND SENT HIM TO HEAVEN!

I lost my dad too.

PETER
Oh, really?

GWEN
Really?

FLASH
YOU WERE CAUGHT OFF GUARD
AND HIT YOU REAL HARD!

PETER
Yeah!

FLASH
LIKE WHEN THE GOVERNMENT DID NINE-
ELEVEN!

GWEN
Ohhhh kay!

FLASH
HERE'S SOME WIT AND WISDOM FROM
HURRICANE FLASH
YOU KNOW, I SUFFERED TOO, LIKE THAT
DRUMMER FROM "WHIPLASH"
YOU NEED A LITTLE COMFORT LIKE BERNIE
SANDERS NEEDS CASH
OH, OH, OH, OH FLASH!
THOMPSON!

Don't get me wrong, I support Bernie.

FLASH (CONT)
(to Gwen)
Always donate to causes you believe in.

PETER
I should be with my aunt.

FLASH
Seek comfort in those close to you, that's natural.

THINGS ARE LOOKING GRIM
HOW CAN YOU BEGIN
TO END THIS MISERY THAT YOU'RE STUCK IN?

GWEN
I don't know where this is going...

FLASH
WHILE YOU'RE ON YOUR OWN
CRYING ALL ALONE
WHILE WE'LL BE TRYING REPRODUCTI--

GWEN
--FLASH! Oh my god, Peter, I'm SO sorry! Flash, lets go!
Now!

Flash and Gwen exit.

SONG 10B. "PETER WHO (REPRISE 2)"

PETER
WHO, PETER WHO?
DON'T KNOW WHAT I'M 'SPOSED TO DO
WHEN LIFE KNOCKS YOU UPSIDE DOWN
JUST GOTTA MAKE IT THROUGH...

PETER crosses into the next scene.

A FEW DAYS LATER.

<u>SCENE 11</u>

INT. 'DAILY BUGLE' OFFICE - DAY

The comic-panel is of the newspaper headquarters, the Daily Bugle.

PETER and BETTY are at the desk with their attention fixed on the Sudoku.

GWEN enters.

GWEN
Peter, sorry to catch you at work, your Aunt May said you'd be here.

PETER
Gwen! Hey, it's fine.

BETTY
Who's this? Peter, we were doing a Sudoku together...

GWEN
Peter, can I talk to you alone for second?

She pulls Peter aside.

BETTY
I'll try to finish all the number 3's for when you get back.

PETER
What's up Gwen, is everything OK?

GWEN

I just wanted to apologize for the other day... At you Aunt's house. It was... inexcusable really... and I feel terrible.

PETER

Don't worry about it. I'm sure he was just trying to help or something.

GWEN

Thanks, but don't make excuses for him, that's a sign of codependency...

BETTY

What's a five letter word for "she's not that much prettier than me?"

PETER

We were doing a Sudoku, not a crossword Betty. Gwen, don't worry about it. And it means a lot that you thought to come here and apologize. How's Chemistry going?

GWEN

OK... well, finals are just a few months away. Are you free Friday? Maybe we can study together, just us?

PETER

Ummm... let me just check my schedule real quick.

Peter calmly walks off stage.

PETER (OFFSTAGE)
YES!! YEEEEES! DEAR SWEET GOD, AWESOME!! THANK YOU!

Peter enters, calmly.

PETER

Yeah, I'm good Friday.

BETTY

So this is what jealousy feels like. Like my soul is being beaten with a sock full of pad-locks.

GWEN

Perfect, see you Friday, Peter Parker.

PETER

Looking forward to it.

GWEN

Me too.

Gwen exits, Peter watches her go.

Betty is isolated with a spotlight.

SONG 10C. "PETER, WHO? (REPRISE 3)"

BETTY

WHO, BETTY WHO?
THE ONLINE DATING STARTS ANEW
THAT LIGHTHOUSE LIGHT IS FADING DARK
NO VACATIONS TO PERU WHO, BETTY WHO?

Jameson enters, lights up to normal.

JAMESON

I heard two girl voices out here! What's going on? I only hired one girl cause that's all that's required by law. You think I'm narrow-minded? Damn right I am! A narrow mind gets fewer headaches! Parker, there's a big story downtown. Killer's on a rampage, also it's the same guy who killed your

JAMESON (CONT)

uncle. Conflict of interest? Sure! But you promised me
you're not a crier! I'll bet money Spider-Man will be all over
it. Get down there and bring me some photos!

LIGHTS CROSS-FADE.

<u>SCENE 12</u>

INT. CHANNEL 4 NEWSROOM - DAY

Split scene: Comic-panel at the TV station, KENT HOLBROOK, who has now been promoted to NY Channel 4, is warming up in his dressing room as assistants are buzzing by.

Other half of the stage is dark.

CAMERA MAN
We're on in thirty.

KENT HOLBROOK
(a vocal warmup)
EMMY, EMMY, EMMY, EMMY!

ASSISTANT 1
You're national now Kent!

KENT HOLBROOK
EMMY, EMMY, EMMY...
THAT'S BECAUSE I WORK HARD
CLARICE... OR LAUREN... OR WHOEVER...

CAMERA MAN
Going live in three... two...

Someone holds an empty comic panel, and Kent stands framed within it.

<u>SONG 11. "KILLER ON THE LOOSE"</u>

KENT HOLBROOK
MY NAME IS KENT HOLBROOK, WITH CHANNEL
FOUR NEW YORK!
IT STARTED AS A ROBBERY
A MAN WAS SHOT AND DIED
HE LEAVES BEHIND HIS NEPHEW AND HIS WIFE

May and Peter jump into the panel, sobbing.

AUNT MAY
Why are you filming me like this?!

They jump off.

KENT HOLBROOK
THE SUSPECT'S NAMED GONZAGO
HE LOOKS A LOT LIKE THIS!

Gonzago briefly jumps into the panel.

KENT HOLBROOK
STAY TUNED AND I WILL HELP YOU SAVE YOUR
LIVES!
MY NAME IS KENT HOLBROOK, WITH CHANNEL
FOUR NEW YORK
PROTECT YOUR CHILDREN, PROTECT YOUR
WIVES.
LOCK YOUR DOORS AND STAY INSIDE
DON'T RUN AND DON'T VAMOOSE
THERE'S A KILLER ON THE LOOSE!

EXT. THE CITY STREETS - DAY

*Lights fade up on the other side of the stage and
down on the TV studio portion.*

The music shifts to the upbeat theme from the Transformation, two ensemble members enter carrying cardboard skyscrapers.

Spider-Man slings through the two buildings, which move behind him and we see a brief portion of Spider-Man pantomiming web-slinging through the skyline but staying mostly center as the two buildings move around him.

Lights then fade down on that side of the stage and back up on KENT in the studio.

INT. CHANNEL 4 NEWSROOM - DAY

KENT HOLBROOK
GONZAGO'S JUST BEEN SPOTTED
ON THIRTY-SIXTH AND PARK
POLICE ARE GIVING CHASE BUT HE'S SO FAST!
THIS IS KENT HOLBROOK, WITH CHANNEL
FOUR NEW YORK.
BE CAREFUL OR TODAY WILL BE YOUR LAST
THIS CRAZY TRAIN'S DE-RAILING
FROM ENGINE TO CABOOSE!
THERE'S A KILLER ON THE LOOSE!

Lights fade down on KENT and up on the other side of the stage.

EXT. THE CITY STREETS - CONTINUOUS

SPIDER-MAN catches up to GONZAGO, the music changes to heavier rock fight music as the thug tries shooting Spider-Man but Spider-Man is too fast.

The two brawl, but Spider-Man bests the criminal and binds him with web.

The fight ends with a Spider-Man delivering a slow motion kick and the thug posing in reaction while they are framed with a comic book panel.

The lights cross-fade back to the studio

INT. CHANNEL 4 NEWSROOM - CONTINUOUS

KENT HOLBROOK
SPIDER-MAN HAS SAVED US
BUT WE'RE NOT SAFE JUST YET
DANGER'S ALWAYS LURKING SO BEWARE!
AGAIN, I AM KENT HOLBROOK, FROM CHANNEL
FOUR NEW YORK
TRUST IN US WE TELL THE TRUTH, I SWEAR.
OUR LIVES WERE SPARED THIS EVENING
PRAISE BUDDHA, GOD, OR ZEUS

But don't get too comfortable...

THERE STILL MIGHT BE A KILLER ON THE
LOOSE!

Music stings.

SCENE 13

EXT. THE CITY STREETS - NIGHT

More time has passed. The stage gets a soft red wash.

Townspeople flood the streets, glued to the newest headlines about "Spider-Man"

Peter, walking home from a hard day crime-fighting, sees everyone glued to the papers.

SONG 11A. "WHO IS THE MAN? (REPRISE)"

A FEW
DID YOU READ ABOUT THE SPIDER-MAN
WHO SAVED THE MAYOR'S DAUGHTER

PETER
Hey, that's my photo!

PERSON
Hey, I'm talking to my FRIENDS!

SOLO
DID YOU READ ABOUT THE SPIDER-MAN
THE POPE JUST CALLED HIS BRO

PETER
I mean I took those pictures--

SOLO
Shut up kid, you're boring!

TWO
DID YOU READ ABOUT THE SPIDER-MAN
I WISH THAT I COULD MEET HIM!

TOWNSPEOPLE
TELL ME WHERE HE COMES FROM
TELL ME NOW, CAUSE I NEED TO KNOW
WHO IS THE MAN?
WHO IS THE MAN, WHO'S HEROICS ARE
INSPIRING?
WHO IS THE MAN?
WHO IS THE MAN, WHO'S SO BRAVE AND
DEATH-DEFYING?

SOLO
I THINK I SAW HIM STOP A ROBBERY DOWN ON
BROADWAY
THAT WAS HAPP'NIN RIGHT IN THE STREET!

TWO
HE WAS RUNNIN' ON THE ROOF TOPS,
HE WAS DANCIN' IN THE SKIES!

A FEW
I ALWAYS THOUGHT A VIGILANTE WAS THE
KINDA GUY
THAT I'D NEVER WANNA MEET!

TOWNSPEOPLE
BUT THIS HERO OF A MAN'S FIN'LY OPENED UP
MY EYES!

SOME LIAR
Spider-Man is gonna do my podcast Thursday!

PETER

Spider-Man is NOT doing your podcast!

SOME LIAR

Shut up! You don't know Spider-Man, nerd! I know Spider-Man!

EVERYONE ELSE
(real impressed)
You do? You know Spider-Man!

Peter steps off to the side.

As he sings the lights isolate him, and the stage is reset around him.

PETER

THINGS ARE CHANGING FOR PETER PARKER
A HEROES LIFE IS A LONESOME RUN
IT'S NOT ABOUT FAME IF I'M CHANGING LIVES
JUST TELL NO ONE... NO ONE...

SONG 11B. "BACK AT CHIPOTLE"

TRANSITION TO:

SCENE 14

INT. CHIPOTLE - EVENING

> *A table is set stage-right with a comic-panel of Chipotle.*
>
> *Lights come up to show PETER and GWEN sitting across from each other. Both have books and note-pads in front of them.*
>
> *There is a WAITER awkwardly standing over them holding a Chipotle bag, the WAITER is 'The One' of the scene.*

PETER
Who'd have thought it would really be great studying at Chipotle?!

GWEN
Their food is fresh, right?

PETER
I know!

> *They notice the creepy waiter.*

GWEN
Are you our waiter?

WAITER
Don't you recognize me yet?

> *They take the bag of food from the Waiter. The waiter leaves, awkwardly.*

GWEN

Um... right.

PETER

OK, section 2, prefix names of covalent compounds. Water?

GWEN

Dihydrogen monoxide.

PETER

Good. Ammonia?

GWEN

Mmm... nitrogen trihydride?

PETER

Yes! NH3, 3 hydrogen atoms! Nice!

>*Gwen casually touches Peter's hand. He get's a little hysterical.*

PETER

Me... Me... Meeee... METHANE?

GWEN

Are you alright? Your hands are all sweaty.

PETER

Oh, I'm just a little nervous... and high strung... probably having an anxiety attack, maybe headed for a stroke, and my pores are huge! Gwen, I feel like a total mess.

GWEN

Everyone's a total mess really... I chew with my mouth open because I don't trust my nose with all the breathing.

PETER

That's smart, never put all your eggs in one basket.

GWEN

I don't eat eggs.

PETER

Good call--

GWEN

--Bird flu.

PETER

--Bird flu.

GWEN

Besides, I don't see any of those things when I look at you...

PETER

I can't imagine what you DO see...

Music starts.

SONG 12. "WHEN I LOOK AT YOU"

GWEN
WHEN I LOOK AT YOU, PETER PARKER
THERE'S A NERVOUS, AWKWARD GUY
ALWAYS SWEATING THROUGH ALL HIS T-
SHIRTS
AND I HAVE TO WONDER WHY
AND WHY WHEN I LOOK AT YOU DO I FEEL THE
WAY I DO?
OH, PETER PARKER, I-

Peter's SPIDEY SENSE goes off.

*Which is the word "tingle" synthesized and
played repeatedly over the speakers.*

PETER
Uh, Gwen hold that thought. I gotta pee.

Peter hurries off.

*Lights go down on the Chipotle date half of the
stage and come up on the other half, a bank.*

INT. A BANK - CONTINUOUS

*The bank is being robbed by ELECTRO who is
taking a giant sack with a dollar sign on it from
a helpless bank teller. The alarm is sounding.*

ELECTRO
Quake with fear at the awesome electrical might of Electro!

*As Electro intros himself, he freezes and
someone holding the comic-book panel runs in
front of him to create an establishing frame.*

*After a beat the comic-book panel is run off and
SPIDER-MAN enters, wearing the famous
Spider-Man suit, finally.*

ELECTRO
YOU'RE TOO LATE SPIDER-MAN,
YOU'RE GONNA EAT MY BLAST
THERE'S A NEW VILLAIN ON THE SCENE!
IT MUST BE FATE, I'M A VICTIM OF A TRAGIC
PAST
AND I'M TELLING YOU WHAT I MEAN!
MY LIFE BEGAN-

Before Electro can launch into his monologue,
Spider-Man quickly beats him to the ground and
goes back to his date. The bank teller takes the
money bag back.

BANK TELLER
Thanks, Spider-Man!

INT. CHIPOTLE - CONTINUOUS

PETER
Sorry, the bathroom line was long.

GWEN
That's ok.

WHEN I LOOK AT YOU, PETER PARKER
WITH YOUR GOOFY, AWKWARD SMILE
THERE IS SOMETHING NEW THAT BEGUILES ME
BUT IT'S TAKEN ME A WHILE
AND WHY WHEN I LOOK AT YOU
DO I FEEL THE WAY I DO?
OH, PETER PARKER, I-

Peter's Spidey Sense goes off again.

PETER
Sorry, I know this is weird but I'll be right back.

PETER exits. The lights cross fade back to the
same bank, which is being robbed again. This
time by SCORPION who is wrestling the money
bag away from the helpless bank teller.

INT. THE SAME BANK - CONTINUOUS

SCORPION

If anyone tries to stop me they'll be crushed by the muscular
tail of the Scorpion!

> *As Scorpion intros himself, he freezes and
> someone holding the comic-book panel runs in
> front of him to create an establishing frame.
> After a beat the comic-book panel is run off and
> Spider-Man enters.*

SCORPION

WELL IF IT ISN'T THE SPIDER-MAN,
WELL TASTE MY TAIL AND HAVE I GOT A TALE
TO TELL!
I MAY BE STRONG NOW
BUT AS A CHILD I WAS WEAK AND FRAIL
IT'S A STORY WE ALL KNOW WELL! MY LIFE
BEGAN-

> *Before Scorpion can launch into his monologue,
> Spider-Man quickly beats him to the ground and
> goes back to his date.*

BANK TELLER

Thanks, Spider-man!

> *The bank teller takes the money bag back. Lights
> fade back up on Chipotle.*

> *INT. CHIPOTLE - CONTINUOUS*

PETER

Thanks for waiting!

> *Spidey sense goes off again.*

PETER

Last time, I swear!

PETER exits, GWEN is alone.

GWEN

AND WHY WHEN I LOOK AT YOU
DO I FEEL THE WAY I DO?
OH, PETER PARKER, I LOVE YOU.

*Lights fade back to the same bank being robbed
yet again, this time by Rhino.*

INT. THE SAME BANK - CONTINUOUS

BANK TELLER

Who are you?

RHINO

RHINO!

*Spider-Man enters and doesn't have the patience
to wait so immediately beats him.*

PETER

Stop! Ruining! My! Date!

*He hurries back to his date. Lights cross-fade,
Peter exits.*

INT. CHIPOTLE - CONTINUOUS

*Gwen is at the table alone, a mysterious figure
sneaks up behind her with a chloroformed rag,
and knocks her out, then carries her off.*

Peter enters to an empty table.

SONG 12A. "PETER, WHO? (REPRISE 4)"

PETER

She left?

> YOU, PETER, YOU?
> I GUESS IT'S CLEAR YOU CAN'T GAIN
> WITHOUT LOSING SOMETHING TOO!

Peter's Spidey Sense goes off again!

SONG 12B. "TO CHAMELEON"

QUICK BLACKOUT.

SCENE 15

EXT. A HIGH-RISE ROOFTOP - TWILIGHT

The comic-panel is the rooftop of a huge building in mid-town at dusk.

GWEN is tied up and CHAMELEON, a soviet spy and master of disguise, is there over her body. He holds an urn.

SPIDER-MAN swings on to save the day.

CHAMELEON
I knew I could get you to come here.

PETER
Who are you? What do you want?

CHAMELEON
I am Chameleon, master of disguise. And you Dr. Spiddermin ARE what I want!

PETER
What are you talking about?

CHAMELEON
Give me the mind-control device, or I will kill this girl in front of you... Can you handle that? Can you handle that guilt? Give me the device!

PETER
I honestly don't know what you're talking about!

CHAMELEON

Don't play stupid with me. I know you are Dr. Kurt Spiddermin, the most brilliant mind in neural science.

PETER

I'm Spider-Man!

CHAMELEON

Yes, yes, Spiddermin.

PETER

Spider-Man!

CHAMELEON

Spiddermin?

PETER

"Spider!"

CHAMELEON

Spidder?

PETER

"Man!"

CHAMELEON

Min?

PETER

Spider-Man.

CHAMELEON

Spiddermin...
(pause)
You can't fool me, I saw you in lab!

PETER

I've never seen you before in my life!

CHAMELEON

But I have seen you. I've been here all along. Don't you recognize-

SONG 12C. "FLASHBACKS"

> *Music swirls, and we see a series of transformation flashbacks to moments in each scene with 'The One'.*

> *These were Chameleon in disguise all along.*

> *Each 'The One' has been played by actors other than the CHAMELEON and as the CHAMELEON swirls around each actor spins with him back to back. High school flashback:*

KAREN

Marvin Keely, I am NOT a patient woman!

> *Marvin smiles at the audience, music swirls and we are on the subway platform:*

FLASH

I always study at Chipotle!

> *The man on the bench smiles at the audience, music swirls and we are in the lab:*

DR. SPIDERMAN

And I've been making Hot Pockets in there all day!

*The Janitor holds his mop smiling at the
audience, music swirls and we are at chipotle:*

GWEN

Are you our waiter?

CHAMELEON

(Moves their lips, but CHAMELEON does the talking)
Don't you recognize me yet!

*Swirling music, back to present day Chameleon
scene, Gwen is still lying on the floor tied up.*

PETER

Pretending to me someone you're not... that's bad karma,
Chameleon!

CHAMELEON

Boo! I have no taste for wit! If you can't give me what I
want, time for death!

PETER

You've got the wrong person. She means nothing to you.

CHAMELEON

Too late for that, I'll have to kill you both. No one sees true
face of Chameleon and lives. Not even my wife!

PETER

You were married? There's hope for the rest of us then!

CHAMELEON

Your one-liners are hurtful to me! You don't know what it is
like... Living like I do... one disguise to the next...

Music starts.

SONG 13. "FACE IN THE MIRROR"

PETER
Please don't tell me about your life.

CHAMELEON
Wearing so many personalities, I forget my own...

PETER
Can we just fight!?

> *The lights fade, there is a thin spotlight on Chameleon's face.*

CHAMELEON
WHAT IS THIS FACE I FACE
WHEN I FACE IN THE MIRROR
I GOT NEW GLASSES YESTERDAY
BUT CAN'T SEE ANY CLEARER
I USED TO KNOW THIS FACE SO WELL
WE'D LAUGH AND CRY AS ONE
BUT THAT FACE GROWS EVER DISTANT
AT THE DIRTY THINGS I'VE DONE
WHAT MAN IS THERE STARING BACK AT ME?
WHOSE FACE IS THIS I SEE?
WHAT IS THIS FACE I FACE
WHEN I FACE MY REFLECTION
I MOISTURIZE IT DAILY
BUT LOOK AT THIS COMPLEXION
IS THIS THE VISAGE OF A VILLAIN
WHO IS RUNNING FROM HIS PAST
OR A MAN WHO SEEKS THE CREDIT
FOR THE THINGS HE'S DONE AT LAST
WHAT MAN IS THERE CALLING OUT THIS PLEA
WHOSE IS THIS FACE I SEE?

CHAMELEON (CONT)
EVERYONE SEES THE FACE OF A MOUNTAIN
OR THE FACE OF THE MOON IN THE SKY
IN AN OPEN-FACED SANDWICH YOU KNOW
WHAT IT IS
WHY NOT I?
WHY NOT I?!

WHAT IS THIS FACE I FACE
WHEN I FACE MY FACEBOOK PICTURES?!
OR FACE A FALSE FACILITY
OF FALLACIES FOR FIXTURES-

> *The music cuts off abruptly.*

> *The lights come up full to reveal that in the
> darkness Peter has untied Gwen and they are
> escaping.*

> *Chameleon pulls a gun.*

CHAMELEON
Hey! What the hell!? Stop right there! I was being sincere
with you and this is how you repay me? You, tie yourself
back up and lay over there! You, prepare to die first!

> *They do as he says, Gwen is re-tied.*

> *Spidey shoots the gun with some web,
> Chameleon charges him and they fight.*

SONG 14. "THE CHAMELEON FIGHT"

> *The CHAMELEON lets out a grunt as he
> charges SPIDER-MAN, the fight music kicks in.*

*They have an epic fight, for a time it looks like
CHAMELEON is overpowering SPIDER-MAN.
Spider-Man lands a hard blow, and Chamleon
transforms into Uncle Ben.*

UNCLE BEN

You could have saved me!

PETER

I'm sorry!

*Uncle Ben knocks Peter down with a volley of
punches. The music changes to down-and-out.
Uncle Ben turns back into Chameleon.*

PETER

Uncle Ben?

CHAMELEON

No, it was me. Doing the thing that I do.

*While the music is slow, Aunt May enters over
Peter's shoulder, spraying her own fog, and
speaking in a ghostly voice.*

AUNT MAY

Be strong for me, Peter! Who's going to help me eat all these
lasagnas?!

*May exits, and the music changes to the upbeat
Spider-Man theme. He rallies, turning the tides,
webs up his enemy, and delivers the knock-out
blow in slow motion as an actor holding the
hollow comic-panel runs on and CHAMELEON
and SPIDER-MAN freeze inside the panel for a
beat creating a tableau.*

The actor and panel exit.

As CHAMELEON hits the floor SPIDER-MAN runs to wake GWEN, as he does so TOWNSFOLK start to enter.

SCENE 16

PERSON

It's Spider-man!

ANOTHER

Look, it's Spider-man!

The townsfolk are causing a hub-bub, and Gwen regains consciousness.

GWEN

Who are you?

PETER

Just your friendly neighborhood Spider-Man!

Peter exits.

GWEN

Wait!

FLASH

My mother loves you Spider-Man!

There is a crowd of people on the street.

They are all excited and talking amongst each other.

Enter Emmy-award winning anchor, Kent Holbrook.

SONG 15. "FINALE"

KENT HOLBROOK
THE CROWDS ARE OUT IN FORCE TONIGHT AND
I CAN TELL YOU WHY.
DANGER HAD BEEN BREWING FOR A WHILE.
A RUSSIAN SPY WAS QUESTING FOR A MIND-
CONTROL DEVICE.
THIS IS KENT HOLBROOK, EMMY STYLE!

He proudly holds up his Emmy Award!

UNLOCK YOUR DOORS, RELEASE YOUR
CHILDREN
BUT KEEP A WARY EYE
CAUSE WE'RE ONLY SAFE
WHILE SPIDER-MAN IS SWINGING THROUGH
THE SKY.

Kent begins to interview the crowd.

FLASH
SPIDER-MAN'S A SYMBOL, HE'S THE HERO THAT
WE ALL NEED!

JAMESON
SPIDER-MAN'S A FRAUD, AN INSTRUMENT OF
CORPORATE GREED!

AUNT MAY
SPIDER-MAN WHO? LOOK EVERYONE I'M ON
TV!

BETTY
SPIDER-MAN IF WANT A LIGHTHOUSE, YOU CAN
FACEBOOK ME!

KENT HOLBROOK
HE IS PROOF YOU CAN MAKE A DIFFERENCE
WITHOUT COMMITTEES AT TOWN HALL
HE WILL BRAVELY RUN
T'WARD THE BLAZING SUN HE'S THE HOPE
INSIDE US ALL!
OH SPIDERMAN'S THE HOPE INSIDE US ALL!

ALL
OH SPIDER-MAN'S THE HOPE INSIDE US ALL!

ONE
I CAN USE A LITTLE HOPE RIGHT NOW

OTHER
I CAN USE SOMEONE TO SET ME FREE

BOTH
WHEN THERE'S DARKNESS ALL AROUND
I NEED A HERO TO HELP ME SEE!
I WANT SPIDER-MAN INSIDE OF ME!

ALL
I CAN USE A LITTLE HOPE RIGHT NOW
I CAN USE SOMEONE TO SET ME FREE
WHEN THERE'S DARKNESS ALL AROUND
I NEED A HERO TO HELP ME SEE!
OH I WANT SPIDER-MAN INSIDE OF ME!
WE CAN ALL USE A LITTLE HOPE RIGHT NOW
WE CAN USE SOMEONE TO SET US FREE
WHEN THERE'S DARKNESS ALL AROUND
WE NEED A HERO TO HELP US SEE!
OH I WANT SPIDER-MAN INSIDE OF ME!
WE CAN ALL USE A LITTLE HOPE RIGHT NOW
WE CAN USE SOMEONE TO SET US FREE
WHEN THERE'S DARKNESS ALL AROUND

ALL (CONT)
WE NEED A HERO TO HELP US SEE!
OH I WANT SPIDER-MAN INSIDE OF ME!
I WANT SPIDER-MAN INSIDE OF ME
I WANT SPIDER-MAN INSIDE OF ME!

SOLO
(Riffing)
I WANT HIM DEEP
SO DEEP!

ALL
OH I WANT SPIDER-MAN INSIDE OF ME!

The ensemble dances their way off, leaving only GWEN.

PETER enters and Gwen goes to him.

GWEN
Peter, you just missed Spider-Man!

PETER
I know! But he told me what happened. I'm sorry about our date, Gwen. I was having a great time.

GWEN
I was too. Maybe we could try again--

Peter's Spidey Sense goes off again!

PETER
Hold that thought! Gwen, sorry, I'll have to call you later.

GWEN
But--

PETER

Sorry!

Gwen exits.

PETER
IT'S MY FATE, NOW I UNDERSTAND
OH, AT LAST, I CAN FIN'LY SEE
THAT WITH GREAT POWER
COMES-

ALL
GREAT RESPONSIBILITY!

BLACKOUT.

SONG 16. "BOWS"

THE END.

www.ingramcontent.com/pod-product-compliance
Lightning Source LLC
Chambersburg PA
CBHW031219120626
46545CB00003B/912